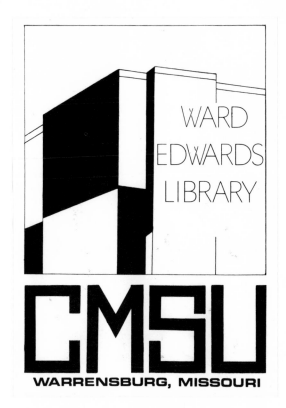

THE NEW ENGLAND IMAGE

THE New

England
IMAGE

BY SAMUEL CHAMBERLAIN

HASTINGS HOUSE, PUBLISHERS   NEW YORK

PUBLISHED 1962 BY HASTINGS HOUSE, PUBLISHERS, INC.

ALL RIGHTS RESERVED

INCLUDING THE RIGHT OF REPRODUCTION

IN WHOLE OR IN PART IN ANY FORM

PUBLISHED SIMULTANEOUSLY IN CANADA

BY S. J. REGINALD SAUNDERS & CO. LTD., TORONTO 2B

PRODUCED IN COLLABORATION WITH CHANTICLEER PRESS, INC., NEW YORK

LIBRARY OF CONGRESS CATALOG CARD NO. 62–13290

PRINTED AND BOUND BY CONZETT & HUBER, ZURICH, SWITZERLAND

FIRST PRINTING

CONTENTS

INTRODUCTION

THE IMAGE OF NEW ENGLAND is a composite of many things—white clapboards in the sunlight, arching elms shading a village street, the pointed spire of an old white church against a clear blue sky. It is found in the silver shingles of Cape Cod, weathered by wind and salt spray, in the curving crescents of sandy beaches, and the clustered masts of fishing boats in Gloucester Harbor. It is reflected in quiet lakes and ponds hidden in the folds of hills and mountains, in the waters of brooks and rivers finding their way to the sea. It is echoed in the austere tones of Cotton Mather calling down through the centuries, and in the beautiful words of Emerson speaking in a Concord church. The poetry of Anne Bradstreet, written three centuries ago in Andover, is filled with praise of this same New England, and the words of those who followed her—Longfellow, Whittier, Lowell, Holmes, Robert Frost—carry the image down through the years.

Beyond question, the artistry of poets surpasses that of photography, a relative newcomer to the New England scene. Yet the observant camera has its own clear interpretation, its own way of telling the story. In the pages that follow, the inquisitive and sympathetic lens will, we hope, capture the essence of this unique corner of our country.

Good pictures have a way of speaking for themselves without fine phrases from their author, and it is with some trepidation that these brief words of introduction have been set down. My alert lens is far more eloquent than my reluctant typewriter, and far better equipped to evoke the New England image, a most elusive phenomenon that I have been pursuing for the past quarter century and more. This book is a condensation of those years of photographing the six New England states in the four seasons of the year. Many of these photographs have never been reproduced before, but scores of others have been chosen from the long list of illustrated books and calendars that have been published by Hastings House during the past twenty-five years.

Perhaps I should begin by recounting the circumstances that launched Hastings House as publishers. It began in the office of the Architectural Book Publishing Company in New York one day in 1935. I had come in for news of my proposed book on small New England houses, the dummy of which I had hopefully left with Paul Wenzel, president of the firm. Mr. Wenzel broke the news gently that this was too far removed from his field, and suggested that I show the book to some other publisher. As I put the dummy in its manila envelope and started to leave, Mr. Wenzel's youthful grandson appeared from the shadows of the stock room and asked if I would have lunch with him. His name was Walter Frese, and it was evident that he had something on his mind.

We went around the corner to a Mexican restaurant, an aromatic place on 47th Street where a bang-up good murder had occurred only a fortnight previously. Over enchiladas and chili, oyster crackers and beer, Mr. Frese admitted that he had suffered acute anguish at the thought of this book escaping from his grandfather's grasp. Moreover, he had long entertained thoughts of launching a publishing house of his own.

"I want to publish this book myself," he confided.

By the time our luncheon was finished, he had the dummy under his arm. In 1936 the book was published as *A Small House in the Sun,* printed in sheet-fed gravure by Photogravure and Color Company. It was the first publication of Hastings House which, in 1961, celebrated its twenty-fifth anniversary. The present volume, still dedicated to the New England theme, was compiled in honor of this quarter century of publishing.

A long list of our illustrated books (thirty-five or so) and calendars (twenty-three) on New England have appeared since that day in the chili parlor. I have worn out a good many cameras, tripods, shoes, and tires in the interval, and the resultant collection of negatives and prints presents a storage problem that has me increasingly baffled and harassed. From this pictorial storehouse, a patient weeding-out process has finally produced the selection of photographs that follows. The omissions are positively monstrous, especially in the field of colleges and famous houses. Space limitations were absolute, however, and we hope that in this limited view the essential beauty and antiquity of New England stand out strong and clear.

All of these photographs, without exception, have been taken with a view camera, using cut film or film packs. The leisurely technique of setting the camera on a tripod, composing the picture carefully on the ground glass, and focusing it sharply under the friendly shelter of a black cloth still seems best to this old-fashioned cameraman, although it can turn into a rather grotesque ceremony on a windy day. One has to put up with the titters and taunts of the school children, and glances of disdain from the average pedestrian. It soon becomes apparent that the status of such a photographer is forlornly low on the social scale. Try invading the campus of a college or preparatory school with tripod, black cloth, and view camera, and you will see what I mean. You will be treated almost like an organ grinder with a monkey. Nor is it easy to climb New England's stone fences with such equipment. On two occasions I have come a cropper on loose stones and crashed with my camera, its bellows distorted in indecent bulges. But the rewards of a sharp, well-composed picture, properly exposed with the aid of a meter, make up for such misadventures.

Another phase of picture-taking calls for less agility and more patience. This is the business of waiting for the sun to come out from behind a cloud after the camera is all set and the shutter cocked. I have often thought of a frightening set of statistics—the number of man-hours that I have expended, standing patient and disconsolate beside my camera, waiting for that triumphant burst of sunlight, without which the picture would have no sparkle.

This leads to the frank admission that this book shows New England in its sunny aspect only. There are plenty of other moods—fog, rain, sleet, and drizzle (but as yet no smog). This is fair weather New England with its best foot set forward, a smiling, beckoning land that brings nostalgic memories to those who have had the misfortune to leave it. The ugly side of the six states has been deliberately sidestepped. We have our grimy factory districts, slum areas, honky-tonk beach communities. Our highways are disfigured by telephone poles and signboards, and black top is creeping over our towns. But this is not a documentary on the bad taste of present-day New England. Rather it is a commentary on the good taste of our ancestors.

Some of these pictures are inevitably dated, and perhaps have a certain historical interest for that reason. Many are taken before television antennae started to lace the rooflines, and parking meters began to pace off the curbstones. The execrable telephone pole, however, has always presented a problem. Heavy with monstrous transformers, crossbars, glass spools and sprawling wires, it ruins many a village landscape and calls for all the artful dodging in the photographer's bag of tricks.

During a quarter of a century many changes take place. Historic buildings burn down. The Wayside Inn at South Sudbury was gutted by fire in 1955, but is now happily restored. Old churches are razed. Fine, venerable farmhouses are covered with artificial brick building paper or phony shingles, monstrosities of this age of fireproofing. Most expendable of all seem to be the wooden schooners that only a few years ago were tied up in various Maine seaports. These have all but vanished. Boothbay Harbor once boasted a half dozen of them, but they have all gone. Two dejected wrecks are still at their pier in Wiscasset as reminders of the great and departed day of coastal schooners.

During these photographic trips I have had many occasions to test the famed New England hospitality, and I can testify to the kindness and friendly interest of the citizens of all six states, particularly in the country towns. In the cities people are too hurried to show much solicitude for a plump party stooping under a black cloth. I've never kept count of the number of times some hospitable person has invited me to lunch or dinner, but it comes to an impressive total. More than once I have been the overnight, and even a week-end guest of perfectly strange people who liked the idea of having their house photographed.

There is another side of the coin, however. Some people violently object to having their house photographed. In most cases of this sort I defer to their wishes and turn my inquiring lens in other directions. Sometimes, however, I stand upon my right to photograph whatever is visible from the public highway, and I have some prints showing an irate man shaking his fist at me,

11

and another showing an indignant woman flapping her arms on her front porch in a determined effort to spoil my picture—which she did. Occasionally I have been attacked by watchdogs, for photographers, along with postmen, have something about them that antagonizes dogs. I've never had my trousers torn off in New England, although this did happen in Italy, and I have mirthful witnesses to corroborate the grievous episode.

Working on this distillation of pictures would have been a totally joyful experience but for one thing—the number of unavoidable omissions that had to be made. How can one deal with the educational facilities of New England in a few chosen pages of pictures? It is quite impossible. Nor can one do justice to old houses, villages, and churches in such a short space. The best we can do is to sketch out the essentials, choosing a few striking examples and those with the greatest historic interest, and apologize for the wealth of subjects that has been left out. In spite of omissions, a true impression of this remarkably beautiful place called New England should be formed.

THE PICTURES have been grouped in a sequence that begins with nature—the four seasons—and ends with nature—the coast from Connecticut to Maine. In between lies a succession of familiar New England institutions—countryside, farms, villages, towns, churches, schools, academies and colleges, old inns, and mills. Finally come the houses, ranging from the cottages of farmers and fishermen to the mansions of opulent merchant princes. The homes of the literary great are here, together with glimpses of doorways and a few interiors. This sequence should permit the image of New England to emerge strong and clear.

Of the four seasons in New England, spring is surely the most welcome, and the most fugitive. It emerges from a time of chill and damp, from bare, leafless branches and brown fields. The faint yellow haze of the willows betrays the first awakening of the sleeping landscape. Almost hidden are the jewels of color where the crocus and daffodil show their heads, followed by the budding green of the elms. Suddenly all is tender green and massed snowy bloom. Apple orchards in southern New Hampshire are dazzling, and the dogwood, both pink and white, brings the visitor out on a Sunday afternoon, particularly in the inland hamlet of Greenfield Hill, Connecticut, where the dogwood trees vault the main road with blossoms.

All too quickly the delicate green darkens. The trees are in full leaf, solid against the hills and sky, and the photographer has a problem on his hands. Summer foliage here is too dense, and photographs black. On Cape Cod and Nantucket, where the roses run riot, he has better luck. And he finds the wind-swept coast of Maine brilliant under a summer sky. This is the season for the vacationist, the motorist from distant parts. Each of the six states has its particular enticements—inland lakes, sandy beaches, mountain resorts. The white sails of yachts flock like birds along the coast, and the summer camps are thronged with happy youngsters.

As compensation for an abrupt spring, New England glories in her long and golden fall. Nowhere are air and light more sparkling, color more brilliant. These are among the most sensational colors in nature, due largely to the extravagant tones of the maple. They range from deep crimson to pale yellow, with every conceivable shade of the spectrum in between. Foliage-conscious motorists make long trips for this spectacle, and camera enthusiasts bedeck their wives with red sweaters and squander rolls of color film. There are signs of harvest—haystacks, corn shocks, and orange pumpkins in the fields. This is a gay season, with back-to-school excitement in villages, preparatory schools, and colleges. It all seems more like a renewal of life than a dying into winter.

Many a New England poet has been inspired by the winter storms of this rugged land. It is a season beloved by skiers and school kids, but mildly cursed by the average New Englander, who swears louder as he grows older. However, this is not a gloomy, overcast winter such as one finds in Northern Europe. It has days of stark, brilliant sunshine, providing a superb opportunity for the well-protected cameraman. The maidenly white birch is his particular delight, and surely the most graceful object in a winter landscape. There comes a somber moment when the snow and ice begin to melt, muddying up the land. Nothing much seems to change in this dull interlude until, suddenly, one morning the willow branches show a faint blush of color. Slowly the cycle begins again.

As farmland, New England's rocky soil cannot be compared to the rich acres of loam in the Middle West. However, rocks can be moved, as the wide stone fences of our farms will prove. The first settlers had no choice but to farm the land, and they struggled valiantly to draw a livelihood from the soil.

New England agriculture can be a phenomenal success, as it is in the tobacco lands of the Connecticut Valley, where cigar wrapper leaf of the finest quality is grown. Long wooden tobacco barns dot this valley. Their vertical sideboards swing open to provide ventilation for the drying leaf. On the other hand, farming can be a bitter struggle for existence, as some of the sparse farms in the Berkshires prove it to be. Italian truck gardeners, accustomed to the austere mountain slopes of their native land, find these rocky acres an easy challenge to their initiative, and they usually win out.

One of our most publicized statistics has it that cattle outnumber people in Vermont. Vast barns proclaim the success of the dairy industry in this state, which deserves to be called the milkshed of New England. Gathering maple sugar is a more picturesque pursuit, and the late winter pictures that show the gathering of the sap and then the boiling down in country sheds are classics of old-time New England. Vermont cheeses age well, and have won wide acclaim among gourmets. Native apple growers do very well indeed. Poultry raising thrives in all six states. It would prosper even more if the New England housewife could be taught more and better ways of cooking chicken.

Even though some farms falter, the old farmhouses linger on after their builders have given up the struggle. They are large structures with commodious barns. They don't resemble Middle Western barns where the buildings are usually scattered. Here in New England, and in Maine particularly, "continuous" farm architecture thrives. This is an arrangement where all the farm buildings are joined together to the house, so that the hardy Maine farmer won't have to go out-

13

doors in zero weather to do his chores and feed his cattle. Today farmhouses are being bought up in increasing numbers by "city people" who seek retirement in a tranquil country setting. Being of sound basic construction, they lend themselves admirably to such a purpose. Rare is the Connecticut farm within commuting distance of New York City that still shelters a farmer.

The perfect New England village is an object of reposeful beauty. It is usually built around a common or green which faces the town hall, the village schoolhouse, and the old white meeting house, together with a few sedate wooden and brick houses set behind prim white fences with ornamental posts. These are the essential elements of the village, together with the grange building and the general store, which often incorporates the post office. Another typical village is built along one wide main street lined with towering elms. The houses are dwarfed by these superb trees which achieve astounding heights of grace and beauty. The elm fits in with man's scheme of life; it grows in the center of his field, along his stone fence and local thoroughfares.

Villages are superb attractions for summer visitors, and we can think of at least twenty-five that any "collector" should not miss. One of our books illustrated a favorite village in each of the six states: Hancock, New Hampshire; Litchfield, Connecticut; Little Compton, Rhode Island; Old Bennington, Vermont; Old Deerfield, Massachusetts; and Wiscasset, Maine. It would be easy to find six close rivals, for example: Orford, New Hampshire; Farmington, Connecticut; Wickford, Rhode Island; Newfane, Vermont; Longmeadow, Massachusetts; and Kennebunkport, Maine.

There are a few old-fashioned industrial villages, built around a factory, that have grown graceful with age. Saylesville, Rhode Island, and Talcottville, Connecticut, are good examples. Old seaports such as Stonington, Connecticut, and Thomaston, Maine, have come through relatively unscathed, and Cape Cod keeps a few villages that have escaped the blight of creeping commercialism; Yarmouthport and Sandwich, for example.

Visitors come in increasing thousands to see the "museum" villages that have developed through the years in New England. Old Sturbridge Village, near Worcester, offers an exciting day to all but the utterly blasé, and especially to children. Old buildings have been assembled around a village green—a church, Quaker meeting house, tavern, general store, print shop, mansion and many other buildings where old-time craftsmen are at work. At Mystic Seaport, in Mystic, Connecticut, a cobbled waterfront street is lined with structures that once would have made up an early seaport, from tavern and counting house to a rope walk and sail loft. Here the last of the old whalers, the *Charles W. Morgan,* has come to rest, and several other notable old vessels ride at anchor.

A remarkable community of old buildings has been assembled in Shelburne, Vermont, under the name of the Shelburne Museum. You may even visit a ferryboat that made an epic overland ride from nearby Lake Champlain. Pioneer Village, in Salem, Massachusetts, gives a good idea of what the earliest settlements on these shores looked like, as does the admirable Plimouth Plantation, now taking form at the landing place of the Pilgrims. The first ironworks in America, dating back to the mid-1600's, has been reconstructed in Saugus, Massachusetts, and the public visits the authentic seventeenth-century house with an Elizabethan overhang, built for one of the original owners of the ironworks. New restorations are being undertaken constantly. Only recently a fine group of old mills and houses in Granby, Connecticut, was opened up as a center of old-time shops and exhibits.

Old Deerfield, Massachusetts, is not strictly a museum village, but a single elm-grown street a mile long, lined with noble old houses, many of which are open to the public. They are beautifully furnished and, during the summer months, receive a large number of enthusiastic visitors who are fabulously repaid for their interest.

The Shaker Village in Hancock, Massachusetts, near Pittsfield, is quite different from the others. This unique community, founded by austere, hard-working, non-mating craftsmen and farmers, has recently been rescued and restored as a museum of early Shaker arts and crafts. Besides an extraordinary circular stone barn, it has a noble collection of buildings and early furniture.

The transition from village to town is often subtle and hard to pin down by definition. One melancholy and inevitable axiom seems to be that the larger the community becomes, the more its artistic purity dwindles. Consequently the seeker of beauty in New England's larger towns and cities must usually search for fragments rather than tasteful ensembles. Fortunately there are exceptions. High Street in Newburyport, Chestnut Street in Salem, Main Street in Nantucket, Benefit Street and its neighbors in Providence, and most certainly Beacon Hill in Boston, are areas where the best of New England taste and architecture has been preserved in depth. In many cases this happy state of affairs has only been achieved by community agreement to preserve historic districts. Other cities have protected their obvious treasures against the inroads of commercialism and ignoble building. New Haven jealously guards its famous Central Green with its three excellent churches. Hartford preserves its old State Capitol designed by Charles Bulfinch. Springfield keeps its historic First Church free from intrusion. Portsmouth, New Hampshire, will reward the summer traveler richly, and so will Newport, Rhode Island, even without its controversial jazz festival. Historical towns have perhaps the strongest appeal of all. The Battle Green in Lexington, the homes of the literary great in Concord, Plymouth Rock and its Plantation are town attractions of extraordinary interest.

Unfortunately there is a less praiseworthy aspect to many New England towns, where historic buildings and landmarks are disappearing before the assault of "progress." A fine brick mansion, built by true craftsmen, is reduced to rubble to make way for a service station. A row of magnificent elms is felled to permit a super-highway to zoom through the town. Black top begins to replace green grass, and jerry-built cinder block buildings give our town business communities the atmosphere of Western tank towns.

There are forces at work against this disintegration. Massachusetts has a "Historic Districts Act" that enables towns to seek protection against the onrush of bad taste and ethics. For many

15

years the Society for the Preservation of New England Antiquities has pioneered in the rescue of historic buildings. It has restored and furnished dozens of imperiled houses, and maintains most of them so that they may be visited by an interested public.

Our sequence of pictures becomes amphibious at this point, digressing to the inland lakes and rivers that wind down to the sea. The Connecticut River is the greatest in New England by far, but there are many others, most of them with intriguing names—the Merrimac, Piscataqua, Kennebec, Penobscot, Housatonic, Thames, and Boston's own Charles. Few of New England's rivers are navigable for any great distance except by small craft and college crews. The smaller rivers provide a reason for a favorite institution, the covered bridge. These are numerous, but their number is being whittled down every year. Fortunately, new wooden covered bridges are being built here and there, so the species is not on the way to total extinction. Sportsmen are happy in New England, for many of its mountain streams are well-stocked with fish. Lakes are not as prodigal here as they are in some of the Middle Western states, but they are sufficiently plentiful in northern New England to make this a favorite summer colony for thousands of vacationists. Lake Winnepesaukee, Sebago Lake, Squam Lake and hundreds of others have their ardent devotees who would never think of spending a vacation anywhere else. Strange Indian names attach themselves to these isolated, pine-bordered lakes, my favorite being Lake Hemquasabamtocook.

A tall white church spire towers above almost every New England community, a symbol of its spiritual consciousness. Architecturally it is usually the most ambitious structure in the neighborhood, and often the most successful. The earliest settlers left their homes in Europe and launched into danger and insecurity to achieve religious liberty. Admirable as this was, it brought its own intolerance with it. The fact that small communities were practically governed by ministers and elders left its mark on the stern, austere little meeting houses that first were built. Many of them had no spire because they were so isolated that a church bell could not be heard by the distant parishioners.

Later generations relented and permitted more gracious structures and today noble old churches, inspired by the English example, are found in many towns. Some reflect the influence of Asher Benjamin or Sir Christopher Wren, although Wren, rumor to the contrary, never designed a New England church. The great Charles Bulfinch left several fine examples, and so did Peter Harrison. The ecclesiastical masterpiece of Samuel McIntire, Salem's great carver-architect, was erected on Chestnut Street in that city, but it burned down in a tragic fire shortly after the turn of the century. Churches are among Boston's greatest attractions with King's Chapel, Old North Church, Old South Church, Park Street Church, Trinity Church, and the first of all Christian Science churches.

There is no rule of thumb in the matter, but the best churches architecturally in New England are likely to be Congregational. The classic Connecticut wooden church has an Ionic portico and a slender spire. There are dozens of examples that closely resemble the one at Litchfield which we illustrate. In Vermont one frequently finds stone churches topped with a white wooden spire, while brick country churches are often found in New Hampshire. Many churches in the country were also used as town meeting houses, and a carriage shed was often built in the rear to protect the horses during deliberations.

The interior of most old churches was chaste and simple. The box pews had mahogany rails, and a delicate Palladian window often brought in light above the pulpit. In settings such as these the voice of religious New England has spoken. Sometimes it echoed the fiery and often bigoted words of early preachers such as Cotton Mather. Later it expressed the liberalism of the Unitarians and the ideas of Ralph Waldo Emerson, or the eloquence of Phillips Brooks, whose sermons in Boston's Trinity Church were world-famous. Our scant few photographs seem sadly inadequate to illustrate a theme as vast as this.

New England's men and women of letters have almost all left houses behind them to keep their memories green. Visitors flock to Concord, Massachusetts, to see the home of Bronson Alcott and his famous daughter, Louisa May Alcott. In the same extraordinary town they find houses where Hawthorne, Emerson, and Thoreau lived for many years. Curiously enough, Hawthorne seems to be the only one to have a faulty sense of architectural fitness. He added an awkward dormer to The Old Manse in Concord, and built a third-story refuge on "The Wayside" that is a genuine disfigurement.

There are three houses closely connected with Longfellow—his birthplace in Portland, Maine, the old brick house in that city where he wrote his first poems, and the imposing house on Tory Row in Cambridge where he lived in later life. Whittier shared most of his life between two houses in Amesbury and Danvers, Massachusetts, while James Russell Lowell saw the first light of day and died in the same mansion in Cambridge. Some people will be surprised to learn that Herman Melville, author of *Moby Dick,* spent much of his life far from the sea in Pittsfield, in western Massachusetts.

Admirers of New England's women poets and novelists have a rare opportunity to see where they produced their work. Sara Orne Jewett's ancestral home in South Berwick, Maine, is open during the summer months. So is the house in Brunswick, Maine, where Harriet Beecher Stowe wrote *Uncle Tom's Cabin.* Also visible is the reserved brick house in Amherst, Massachusetts, where the lonely and mysterious Emily Dickinson lived and wrote her exquisite poems. Recent researchers have cast some doubt upon the so-called Anne Bradstreet House in North Andover, Massachusetts, contending that it is not early enough to have been her home. Be that as it may, the first woman poet in America certainly lived in this village in a location approximately the same as this venerable house.

It is in the domain of education that New England's pre-eminence is most pronounced. Education has been a prime pursuit since the days of the Pilgrims. The Englishman's love of learning came with him from across the sea. He brought a few precious books with him, and lost no time in building schools. Harvard College, the oldest in this country, was founded in Cam-

17

bridge in 1636, and by the middle of the eighteenth century many small colleges were thriving in the New England area. Small academies founded in single brick schoolhouses grew into such great preparatory schools as Andover and Exeter. The old academic buildings built in the 1600's have disappeared, but there are noble survivors from later centuries, particularly at Harvard, Yale, Brown, Dartmouth, Bowdoin, Williams and Amherst. In recent decades educational institutions have undergone such rapid growth that ancient, ivy-clad walls are becoming a rarity. Education at all levels is in a ferment of healthy and vigorous growth at this moment. New colleges are cropping up, immense building projects are under way, fund raising in multiple millions is going ahead by giant strides. Now there are six state universities in addition to a prodigious number of privately endowed higher institutions of learning, making New England, beyond any doubt, the most sought-after educational center in the country. A plump illustrated volume could be written on this subject alone, and these few pages can only skim the surface.

Venerable coaching houses and inns are still standing on post roads in many parts of New England. You will find them as far afield as Machias, Maine, where the old Burnham Tavern was built in 1770. Some of them still welcome guests for an overnight stop, although visitors arrive in anything but a stagecoach today. Many have been adapted as restaurants and taverns, and some of them serve food on a par with New England's best. One of the most famous is the Wayside Inn, made known by Longfellow's tales. It has undergone many changes and misfortunes, but it is now restored, and welcomes visitors from every part of the country. Lexington has two famous inns. One of them, the Buckman Tavern, faces the Battle Green, and served as a rendezvous for the Minutemen. The Munroe Tavern, at the other end of the village, was occupied by the British commander, Earl Percy, on that fateful day of April 19, 1775.

New England has been a manufacturing region since the early days when mills, foundries, and small factories flourished in the seventeenth century. Mill dams along streams and rivers are still numerous, marking the site of once thriving manufacturing plants. Many of these early factories have vanished with time, but it is still possible to see how they once looked. The Saugus Ironworks, first in America, has been reconstructed on its original site, just as it appeared in the 1640's. The first cotton thread mill in America is still standing in Pawtucket, Rhode Island, and may be visited. We show these and a handful of others, forerunners of the factories that, alas, do little to beautify the New England scene today. But they make a mighty contribution to the economy, and one has only to visit Bridgeport or Worcester to appreciate the fact.

The development of the house, from thatched hut and pitch-roofed farmhouse to the luxurious three-story mansion, is one of the most revealing and personal phases of the New England image. Old houses are inextricably tied up with the life and drama of this land from the first epochal days at Plymouth to the proud moment when it emerged from the Revolution, a vital part of the brave young Republic. The lives of our ancestors, the personalities of our noted men of history, are vividly revealed by the houses they lived in.

18

Only at the dawn of Colonial New England did the Pilgrims and the earliest pioneers content themselves with rough shelters. These consisted of a large fireplace, to which was attached a crude one-room dwelling with a garrett and a steep roof, often thatched. If more room was needed, a similar habitation was added to the other side of the fireplace. Immediately following the first pioneers came hardy settlers from England, intent upon building substantial homes in this new land. Many of them were fine craftsmen, carpenters and masons, and they erected traditional wooden manor houses, precisely as they had done at home. The Parson Capen House in Topsfield, Massachusetts, is a perfect example of this so-called Elizabethan style. These houses had ornamented overhangs, steep roofs, and leaded casements. But they proved imperfectly adapted to local conditions, which included hostile Indians, different building materials, and a more rigorous climate.

A more local style of architecture soon evolved. Its usual arrangement consisted of a house of four rooms, two upstairs and two down, all clustered about a huge central chimney of stone or brick. Between the two lower rooms was a narrow entrance hall, and a steep stairway clung to the chimney. The floors of the upper rooms were supported by huge "summer" beams resting on the chimney and the outside wall.

As the early Colonial family grew, wings and ells were added to provide added rooms for children. A "lean-to" was also frequently built. This carried the rear roof closer to the ground and provided more room, usually for an enlarged kitchen. Thus the "salt-box" type was created. At first the lean-to was an aftermath of marriage, so to speak, but later it became a built-in feature of new houses. A few dwellings at this time were built, not around a central chimney but between two massive ends of brick or stone.

As peace and prosperity came to the colonists, their homes took on more amplitude and distinction. New houses were built with four and five rooms on each floor instead of only two. In place of one central chimney there were two, each with fireplaces to heat two rooms, upstairs and down. Between them ran a spacious central hall. In plan these new larger houses were really a pair of two-room houses of the early period, turned sideways and separated by a hallway. The houses were nearly square, and gambrel and hip roofs had to be designed to cover the increased span. Leaded windows gave way to double-hung sashes with small wooden muntins. Fine carpentry, good paneling, and delicately detailed doorways and mantels became evident in the mansions of the wealthier citizens. Walls were plastered now, and ceiling beams were concealed.

After the architectural lull of the Revolution, a new sophistication began to seep in from Europe. Our carpenters and wood workers studied books of measured drawings from England, and were especially enamored of the works of Asher Benjamin. The influence of Sir Christopher Wren and the Brothers Adam began to be felt in the new Republic. The central hall plan led to better balanced houses, more formal and imposing. Ceiling heights lifted and entrance doorways became more pretentious, embracing transoms and sidelights. The use of paneling became less common, and cameo-like Adam mantelpieces appeared. The three-story mansion arrived im-

19

pressively, its best expressions being in the exquisite designs of Charles Bulfinch, the Boston architect, and Samuel McIntire, the carver-architect of Salem.

The subject of New England doorways can fill a book by itself. In fact, we published one in 1939. The doorway and the fireplace were focal points of interest in the early houses, places where the builder might ignore stern necessity for a moment and indulge his desire for ornament. Our little four-page selection gives a brief glimpse of the skill and good taste that the early craftsmen lavished upon the doorway.

For a few pages the scene shifts beyond New England thresholds, where the hearth becomes the central theme. From pioneer days life was centered about the fireplace, principal source of warmth, nourishment, and cheer. Under the huge, hand-hewn lintel the housewife kept pots stewing and spits turning. In its brick ovens she baked her corn bread and beans and Indian pudding. On wintry nights its roaring blaze warmed the whole family, huddled close in high-backed settles. The broad lintel gave way in time to a smaller fireplace framed in paneling that became more refined as time went on. With increased prosperity and fastidiousness, the New England interior took on new refinement, culminating in the exquisite carving of Samuel McIntire and the opulence of such mansions as Gore Place in Waltham, Massachusetts, and Linden Place in Bristol, Rhode Island.

From this praiseworthy pinnacle, American domestic architecture disintegrated by degrees, pausing in its downward path to indulge in some interesting Neo-Classic impulses. The decadence of house design became increasingly evident, and ended in a complete debacle in the late nineteenth century. During this time our old houses were looked upon with indifference, if not scorn, and many splendid examples were torn down. Fortunately the pendulum of appreciation began to swing back during the first years of the twentieth century. Old houses were rescued from oblivion, restored and furnished, and often opened to the public as "house museums."

From a pictorial point of view, the coastal part of New England is most gratifying of all, especially to painters, etchers, and the inevitable cameramen. Yachtsmen and summer vacationists share the same enthusiasm. In the hope of achieving a final flourish, we propose a short guided tour of this varied coastline, beginning in Connecticut where Mystic Seaport sets an impressive pace. Here many noble vessels are tied up at their final mooring, and the life of an old seaport town is dramatized for countless visitors. This is beyond doubt the stellar attraction along the Connecticut shore, but there are bathing beaches and yachting centers all along Long Island Sound from Greenwich eastward to Stonington, a splendid old seaport that shouldn't be missed.

The eccentric shores of Rhode Island provide the inquisitive motorist with a remarkable tour around Narragansett Bay, including a visit to plutocratic Newport and its outdated palaces. Along the way is the charming village of Wickford, while Bristol, on the road to Mt. Hope Bridge, is an aristocratic town of great architectural distinction.

Next come the famous islands that lie south of Cape Cod. Martha's Vineyard is the largest and most dramatic, as a glimpse of Gay Head at sunset will prove. Nantucket is farther out in the immensity of the Atlantic, a romantic outpost that was once the world's greatest whaling port. Visitors from our inland states are always intrigued by these two islands, both of which are superbly equipped as summer resorts. Cape Cod has the same magnetic charm, but it is threatened by commercialism, especially along its south shore. A vital part of this great hooked peninsula will probably be saved for posterity, thanks to the Department of the Interior, which has proposed a Cape Cod National Seashore running from Chatham to Provincetown.

The remainder of the Massachusetts shoreline is studded with interesting ports. We touch only the high spots from Plymouth, landing place of the Pilgrims, to Boston, international port and mooring place of "Old Ironsides," which rests in the Charlestown Navy Yard. North of Boston are Marblehead, yachting capitol of New England; Rockport, the favorite of summer artists; and Gloucester, foremost of our fishing ports.

New Hampshire's share of the coast is modest, a stretch of twenty miles or more. But much of it is sandy beach, and hence popular with summer visitors. A few immense seaside hotels prosper here, especially geared to large conventions.

Coastal Maine, of course, is astonishing. It measures almost twenty-five hundred miles in length, not counting the archipelago of some four hundred offshore islands. Between Kittery, on the north bank of the Piscataqua River and West Quoddy Head, the easternmost point in the United States, the visitor will find just about everything to stir his imagination—old fortresses, famous lighthouses, fishing villages, yachting centers, artist's colonies, lobstermen's settlements piled high with slatted lobster pots. There are innumerable resorts with inviting beaches, summer theaters and enticing shops. This is one of the coolest places in the country to spend the hot season, and summer residents are numbered in the thousands.

This inquiring camera attempts to provide a farewell glimpse of the charms of the Maine shore, but frankly there is only one way to appreciate its beauty—by going there yourself. You will find that the image of New England is never more radiant than along its coast on a bright summer day.

Samuel Chamberlain

THE NEW ENGLAND IMAGE

"If we had no winter, the spring would not be so pleasant: if we did not sometimes taste adversity, prosperity would not be so welcome."

ANNE BRADSTREET, *circa 1688*

This broad panorama begins with
THE FOUR SEASONS IN NEW ENGLAND,
and shows spring, the most fugitive of the four, as it bedecks
the southern New Hampshire village of Hudson.

Early spring in Wickford, one of the most beguiling of Rhode Island villages. The forsythia is in bloom, but only a trace of bud is visible on the elms. Wickford takes pardonable pride in its many well-preserved 18th-century houses.

Magnolia is in full bloom in the Connecticut village of Greenfield Hill *(opposite)*. Its dogwood trees, pink and white, arch the roadway for a short fortnight of blossom, at which time the little place is thronged with sightseers.

Spring shows Thomaston, Maine, sprucing up its small craft for the boating season ahead. A trading post stood here in 1630, and successfully beat off Indian attacks.

Boothbay Harbor, Maine, is a reminder that summer is symbolized by the water. A float, a sailboat, and a skyline jagged with evergreens—this means summer to countless New Englanders. Boothbay Harbor has always been popular with artists, playwrights, and yachtsmen.

A calm, unruffled afternoon in Northwood, New Hampshire, produced this portrait of New England summer. The farmhouse is unmistakably Yankee.

Three trees, a stone fence, and a fine summer sky make up a typical Connecticut landscape near Woodbury. Rembrandt made an etching of three trees, and we don't pretend that the camera can do as well.

Summer on a Vermont farm, near North Thetford. The barn is crowned by a Victorian cupola, the hallmark of most barns in the upper Connecticut Valley.

The town of Portsmouth, Rhode Island, could once be proud of its old shingled windmill, a survivor of many that stood on a hilltop above Narragansett Bay. But it has fallen into disrepair during the years, and no longer presents this silhouette. The first settlement at Portsmouth was in 1638, when nineteen colonists migrated from Massachusetts Bay Colony.

Autumn turns the maples to flaming gold and crimson on this Yankee farm near Newport, New Hampshire.

Autumn in the White Mountains. Mount Chocoura, framed in yellow-leafed birches, is one of the most photographed spots in New Hampshire.

All is quiet on this leaf-clad hillside near Lower Waterford, Vermont, but when maple sugar time comes this will be a busy place.

32

Harvest time near Hadley, Massachusetts, in the Connecticut Valley. New England's output of corn is modest compared to Iowa's, but some nice landscapes result.

Hillside birches on an October day in Vermont. The rough and ready Green Mountain Boys, whose chief was Ethan Allen, roamed over these hills during Revolutionary days. The Battle of Bennington was fought nearby.

A winter morning on a well-swept side road in Beverly, Massachusetts. The towering elms take on a delicate silver tracery.

34

The rhythm of winter, expressed in this flow of branches, snow, and shadow, was found on a roadside near Topsfield, Massachusetts.

Litchfield, Connecticut, a New England town of exceptional charm, is even lovelier under a mantle of snow. Settled in 1720, Litchfield was named after the old cathedral town in Staffordshire, England. Ethan Allen; Henry Ward Beecher, the famous preacher; and his even more famous sister, Harriet Beecher Stowe, were all born here.

Mount Anthony, Old Bennington, Vermont.

NEW ENGLAND FARMS are usually modest in scale. This one near Dresden Mills, Maine, is dwarfed by a magnificent spreading elm.

Unique in farming New England is the immense circular stone barn built in Shaker Village, Hancock, Massachusetts, by a disappearing sect. The entire farm is now being restored as a living museum.

Life on this Vermont farm near Manchester *(opposite)* is sluggish during the winter months. Cattle gather morosely beside the red barn and wait for spring.

The Connecticut River Valley produces the finest wrapper tobacco for cigars. It is dried in well-ventilated sheds, such as these near Rockville.

Life on a backwoods farm in the Berkshire hills is stern business. The weather is rugged, the land not too fertile, and the demands put upon the farmer are heavy. This group is in Hancock, Massachusetts.

The most perfectly preserved of New England's windmills *(opposite)* is in the Cape Cod village of Eastham, settled in 1644. It dates from 1793, and was restored by the WPA in 1936. A custodian shows the ancient machinery for grinding corn.

We're not sure about the statistics in New Hampshire, but it is well known that cows outnumber human beings in Vermont. These animals in a pasture near Tamworth, New Hampshire, view the photographer with more disdain than curiosity.

Small iron mines were once a part of New England industry. This old iron smelter at East Dorset, in the Vermont hills, was expertly built with marble scraps from a nearby quarry, now abandoned. The New York Public Library is built of marble from this area.

President Calvin Coolidge was born on Independence Day, 1872, in this crossroads country store in the hamlet of Plymouth, Vermont. He was here with his familiy when news of President Harding's death came on August 3, 1923, and was sworn into office by his father at 2 A. M. on the worn family Bible. He lies buried in a hillside cemetery in his native village.

42

The camera can find rhythm in something as mundane as a wood-pile, as we've tried to prove with this willowy composition on the grounds of the Old Witch House in Pigeon Cove, Massachusetts.

This isolated Cape Cod privy in North Truro, Massachusetts, took on dramatic overtones when a dead tree fell next to it.

The autumn sky is menacing over this farm in South Monmouth, Maine, but a flash of late afternoon sunshine makes the white farmhouse glitter.

A prosperous farm near Ely, Vermont, at harvest time. The distinguishing cupola marks the barn as belonging to the Connecticut Valley.

THE NEW ENGLAND VILLAGE is often built around an elm-shaded green, dominated by a prim white church. New Marlboro, in the Berkshires, was once on the stagecoach
route between Hartford and Albany, and still retains its Old Wayside Inn.

Stark, New Hampshire, a most photogenic village on the banks of the Upper Ammonoosuc River, has a fine covered bridge. It is named in honor of General John Stark, who gained fame in the Revolution.

The general store at Waterford, Maine *(opposite),* dappled with sun and shadow, is a hospitable place with two curved benches provided for village philosophers.

The crossroads village of Stoddard, New Hampshire, is colorful in the full flush of autumn. A Civil War monument stands stiffly in front of the church.

The Cape Cod cottage, still the most popular residential motif in New England, is sometimes shingled, sometimes sided with clapboards. These are authentic old ones, bordering the road in Yarmouthport, Massachusetts.

The village green in Newfane, Vermont *(opposite),* serves as a perfect setting for the local World's Series. Eugene Field, the poet, spent several boyhood summers in this village, and recalled his youthful days in later poems.

A good deal of architectural style is evident in this village street at Kingston, Rhode Island, an isolated and unspoiled college town.

Old Sturbridge Village, a typical settlement as it might have appeared in the early 1800's, has been assembled on farm lands near Sturbridge, Massachusetts. Old buildings have been moved from near and far—stores, houses, schools, and shops of craftsmen who demonstrate their skills before attentive visitors. Farmhouses, country inns, and an old grist mill are among the attractions of this living museum, which has become known to visitors from all over the world. Above is a group comprising the Deneson School, Miner Grant's General Store, and at the head of the Green, the village mansion built by Salem Towne. At the left is the Meeting House, standing at the end of a wintry landscape.

Mystic Seaport, a community of another kind, has sprung up in recent years on the site of old shipyards at Mystic, Connecticut. The streets of an early New England seaport come alive once again—the general store, of course, but also the waterfront counting house, the tavern, sail loft, rope walk, ship-smith shop: all rich reminders of life in a seafaring town. Many famous ships are now moored at the Mystic docks, including the training ship *Joseph Conrad;* the last of the great whalers, *Charles W. Morgan;* and the *Bowdoin,* veteran of twenty voyages to the Arctic.

Kennebunkport, Maine, an elm-shaded resort village of great charm, is a favorite with authors, artists, and "summer people." Booth Tarkington, Margaret Deland, and Kenneth Roberts all lived here.

The mile-long street in Old Deerfield, Massachusetts, is lined with dignified old houses, at least ten of which are open to the public. Two of the most ghastly massacres of our early history almost wiped out this frontier village in the 17th century, but it is now revived and serene, safely by-passed by the highway.

Surprisingly few houses are built of stone in rocky New England. The answer is that wood was also plentiful, and cheaper and easier to handle. The little town of Chester Depot, Vermont *(opposite)*, is an exception to the rule. A large part of the village is built of native stone.

The white-steepled Town Hall at Chesterfield, New Hampshire, reminds one of a small New England church. The distinguished native son of this village was Harlan Fiske Stone, Chief Justice of the United States Supreme Court.

52

This antique shop in Essex, Massachusetts, has much of the atmosphere of an old-time country store. The temptation to buy a hooked rug at a bargain price is too strong for many a tourist.

Another assembled community of old New England buildings is the Shelburne Museum in Shelburne, Vermont. The entrance is through a covered bridge, guarded by immobile steeds. Besides finely furnished old houses, shops, and craftmen's workrooms, visitors may also see a displaced lighthouse and the veteran ferryboat *Ticonderoga,* which is now landlocked after a sensational overland trip from the borders of Lake Champlain.

Main Street in a NEW ENGLAND TOWN has great charm in some cases, and commercial desolation in others. Woodstock, Vermont, belongs in the first category. Favored first by sedate summer residents and then by a gay band of youthful skiers, it also has a town life all its own. The vintage automobiles date this picture somewhere in the early forties.

One of the most prosperous of New England towns in Colonial days, Portsmouth, New Hampshire, was a town of fine mansions with dignified doorways. Many of them have lived on intact, partly because prosperity retreated after the Revolution and the impoverished owners could not afford to tear them down and build 19th-century monstrosities. In the foreground of this group on Middle Street is the Langley-Boardman House, built about 1805.

A lively and graceful statue of Commodore Oliver Hazard Perry *(opposite)* looks over Washington Square in downtown Newport, Rhode Island. This is the older and less social part of this famous resort, where sailors are a more frequent part of the landscape than dowagers.

At the top of Chapel Street in Portsmouth is St. John's Church, built in 1807, whose church bell was taken from the French at Louisburg in 1745 and recast by Paul Revere. Among the pew owners were Benjamin Franklin and Daniel Webster.

Often called the most beautiful street in America, Chestnut Street in Salem, Massachusetts, is lined with stately three-storied mansions built by rich, intrepid young sea captains and merchant families in the early 19th century. The wide avenue is arched with elms, and dates from 1796. Telephone poles are banned, one reason for its beauty.

Historical precedent, following closely the Bulfinch tradition, has been observed in this group of town buildings in Clinton, Connecticut (opposite), a quiet coastal town named for Governor De Witt Clinton of New York.

In the foreground of this winter view of Chestnut Street is the Captain Jonathan Hodges House, the only house on the street designed by Salem's great carver-architect, Samuel McIntire.

On the crest of the Common in Wiscasset, Maine *(opposite)*, is the Meeting House and the Lincoln County Courthouse, whose courtroom often echoed to the oratory of Daniel Webster.

New England's most famous Common, the Battle Green in Lexington, Massachusetts, is marked by a boulder inscribed with the words of Captain Parker's immortal command.

County courthouses are not always objects of beauty, but the Windham County Courthouse in Newfane, Vermont, has great charm, reflected as it is in a fountain on a golden autumn day.

Most of the gravestones have disappeared from the Federal Street Cemetery, a half-forgotten burial ground in Wiscasset, Maine. The earliest tombstone is that of Joshua Pool, whose canoe capsized in the nearby Sheepscot River in 1739.

THE RIVERS AND LAKES OF NEW ENGLAND could fill a volume by them-
selves. What follows is a mere sampling, beginning with the mouth of the Parker River, near
Newbury, Massachusetts, on an idyllic summer day.

This old covered bridge at Groveton, New Hampshire, has been supplanted by a modern one, and is now preserved as a museum reminder of the good old days. Paper making is the major industry of the town, and large piles of pulp logs are heaped on the right.

The Connecticut River *(opposite)*, longest and greatest in New England, forms the boundary between New Hampshire and Vermont, and runs from near the Canadian border to its outlet at Old Saybrook, Connecticut. This view was taken near White River Junction, Vermont.

An old wooden mill with a water wheel stands beside Podunk River Falls, near East Windsor, Connecticut. Podunk was the name of an Indian tribe before it came to be applied to jerkwater towns.

The Charles River, which separates Boston from Cambridge, is particularly attractive at this point where Harvard's Lowell, Leverett, and Dunster houses rise up from its banks. The profile has not been improved by some recent skyscraper dormitories.

The combination of a covered bridge and a river plunging over the rocks *(opposite)* is irresistible to the passing photographer. The bridge was too good to last, however, and this veteran at Barnet, Vermont, has given way to a cold, concrete successor.

The river town of Warren, Rhode Island, presents a silhouette of old waterfront buildings and church towers that has changed but little in the past century. This is taken from the Barrington bank of the Warren River.

The State of Maine is spotted with thousands of inland lakes, beribboned by many rivers, and bordered by the most jagged coastline in the country. This spot near Gardiner is one of the reasons that "Vacationland" appears on the state license plates.

Twenty-two miles long and very complex in shoreline, Lake Winnipesaukee (there are 132 different spellings of the name) is one of the most popular of New Hampshire lakes *(opposite)*. It is said to possess an island for every day of the year, and 274 of them are habitable. Its waters are stocked with salmon, trout, black bass, horned pout, and other smaller fry.

The covered bridge, one of the most cherished of New England institutions, is disappearing little by little—victim of highway expansion, old age, and public indifference. This sturdy veteran is in Ashuelot, New Hampshire.

Only the ducks ruffle the still waters of this mill pond in South Gouldsboro, Maine.

THE CHURCHES OF NEW ENGLAND symbolize the spiritual life of this deeply religious part of America. A beautiful example is the Old Meeting House (1816) that faces the Common in Lancaster, Massachusetts. The Greek influence is already visible in this church, perhaps the finest of those designed by Charles Bulfinch.

71

Christ Church, the oldest in Cambridge, was built in 1761 from designs by Peter Harrison. Its fine interior is a rare example of Georgian Colonial architecture. Many famous people have worshipped here, including George and Martha Washington. During the Revolution the pipes from the organ were melted into bullets.

Built in 1723, the interior of Christ Church *(opposite)*, in Boston's North End, is influenced by designs of Sir Christopher Wren. Each box pew is marked by a small brass plate carrying the names of 18th-century owners, usually prosperous merchants. This church is better known as the Old North Church, in whose belfry the two lanterns made famous by Paul Revere were hung at the outbreak of the Revolution.

Trinity Church, facing Boston's Copley Square, was built in 1877 and is considered the crowning achievement of the great architect, H.H. Richardson. It is inspired by 11th-century churches built in the French Auvergne province. The eloquent preacher, Phillips Brooks, spoke from this pulpit for many years, and a statue of him by Augustus Saint-Gaudens stands beside the church.

73

The Old Narragansett Church, built in the 18th century, occupies a quiet setting in Wickford, Rhode Island. Externally it is rather severe, without a tower of any sort, but the doorway and windows are delicately detailed. The old slave pews may still be seen in the gallery.

A perfect example of the classic white Connecticut church *(opposite)* faces the green in Litchfield. It was built in 1829, and has several close counterparts in the state. The graceful steeple has two octagonal stages and terminates with a slender cone.

Three famous churches are set on the broad Central Green at New Haven, Connecticut. In the middle distance is Center Church, built in 1812–14 by Ithiel Town, who was obviously inspired by St. Martin's-in-the-Fields in London. In the background is the United Church, built about the same time by David Hoadley. Not in the picture is Trinity Episcopal Church, a dignified Gothic Revival edifice.

The old meeting house erected in Hancock, New Hampshire, in 1820, serves both as a church auditorium and, on the ground floor, a town office. The semi-circular carriage shed for horse-drawn vehicles casts a long, sweeping shadow. This is probably the finest shed of its kind in New England. In the tower hangs a bell bearing the Revere family name.

The Old Round Church *(opposite)*, built in Richmond, Vermont, in 1803, is actually sixteen-sided, topped with an octagonal belfry. Originally built as a joint undertaking of five religious sects, it eventually became the town hall.

The Martha Mary Chapel rests on the crown of a gentle hill on the property of the Wayside Inn at South Sudbury, Massachusetts.

Here is the essence of coastal Maine—a sunny little wooden church, and a stark white house, silhouetted against the blue water at Castine. The church dates from 1790 and is one of the oldest in Maine.

The Congregational Church *(opposite)* in the charming college town of Middlebury, Vermont, was built in 1806–09, and is based on a design by Asher Benjamin.

One of the best of the Victorian wooden Gothic churches that blossomed forth in the 19th century sits on a hilltop in Ipswich, Massachusetts.

LITERARY NEW ENGLAND can be pictured by the houses where its illustrious poets and authors lived. John Greenleaf Whittier, whose poems reflect the very essence of New England, lived at Oak Knoll, in Danvers, Massachusetts, from 1876 until his death in 1892.

81

At this hillside farm called "Fruitlands," A. Bronson Alcott, Transcendentalist author and father of Louisa May Alcott, attempted to create a "new Eden" in Harvard, Massachusetts. Even with the help of the English mystics the attempt failed.

This simple Georgian house at South Berwick, Maine, is the birthplace of the noted Maine authoress, Sarah Orne Jewett. It was built in 1774, and purchased by her grandfather, Captain Theodore Jewett. Her father was a doctor, and the background for one of her best novels, *A Country Doctor,* was based on his experiences. Her best-known work, published in 1896, is *The Country of the Pointed Firs.*

Orchard House in Concord, Massachusetts, was the home of A. Bronson Alcott and his family for twenty years. They repaired and painted it themselves. It was here that Louisa May Alcott wrote the first part of *Little Women*. Visitors may see the room where she worked, and visualize more clearly the story of Jo, Meg, Beth, and Amy.

The Old Manse, a large gambrel-roofed homestead built by Concord's fighting minister, Reverend William Emerson, is near the famous North Bridge that crosses the Concord River. The minister's grandson, Ralph Waldo Emerson, spent many happy days here as a schoolboy, and later lived here for a year. Nathaniel Hawthorne rented the house in 1842 and brought his bride to live here for four years.

Ralph Waldo Emerson built this square white house in Concord, Massachusetts, in 1835, and lived here until his death in 1887. During this time a long succession of famous visitors crossed the threshold. Thoreau occupied the house during one of Emerson's European trips. The poet's study has been moved intact to fireproof quarters in the Antiquarian House across the road.

84

The House of the Seven Gables in Salem, Massachusetts, has always been associated with Nathaniel Hawthorne and his famous novel by that name. His spinster cousin, Susan Ingersoll, lived in this old Elizabethan house built in 1668, and Hawthorne was one of the few men permitted to cross the threshold. He wrote *The Scarlet Letter* in Salem, but *The House of the Seven Gables* was written in a cottage in the Berkshires. Hawthorne once served as the surveyor of the Port of Salem, and his desk at the Custom House is still in place.

Nathaniel Hawthorne was born in this Salem house in 1804. It has recently been restored and moved to a spot near the House of the Seven Gables.

Anne Bradstreet, the first American woman of letters, has been associated with this saltbox house in North Andover, Massachusetts. She was born in England in 1612, the daughter of Thomas Dudley, who later became Governor of Massachusetts. Coming to New England in 1630 with her husband, Simon Bradstreet, she produced seven children and enough poems to earn high praise from the early colonists. *Contemplations* was considered one of her best poems.

Emily Dickinson, the poet, was born, lived, and died in this brick house in Amherst, Massachusetts. It was built in 1813 by her grandfather. This mysterious recluse, who wandered in her father's garden dressed in white, has won recognition as one of America's great poets. Practically all of her poems were published after her death in 1886. A replica of the room where she wrote is now in the Houghton Library at Harvard.

"Elmwood," the westernmost of the seven great mansions on Tory Row in Cambridge, was the birthplace of James Russell Lowell, poet, essayist, and ambassador to the Court of St. James. This house was built in 1767 by Thomas Oliver, the unpopular last royal deputy in Massachusetts. During the siege of Boston it was occupied by Benedict Arnold and his company, and later by Vice-President Elbridge Gerry, whose family sold it to the father of James Russell Lowell. Here the poet produced most of his work.

This house in Brunswick, Maine, was the home of Harriet Beecher Stowe at the time she wrote *Uncle Tom's Cabin*. It is located on a side street near Bowdoin College, where her husband held a professorship. She was the mother of six children, some of whom were born in Brunswick.

The Vassall-Craigie-Longfellow House in Cambridge was built in 1759 by an ardent Royalist, Major John Vassall. Later it was used by George Washington during his stay in Cambridge. Henry Wadsworth Longfellow roomed here first as a Harvard instructor. Later he acquired the house, and brought his second bride here.

The William Cullen Bryant House in the Berkshire town of Great Barrington, Massachusetts, was also built in 1759. This is the scene of the poet's courtship and marriage, and here the young couple lived for several years. The poet was performing the mundane duties of town clerk at the time.

88

Every American schoolboy knows the lines written by Longfellow about the Old North Church in Boston: "One, if by land, and two, if by sea; and I on the opposite shore will be." Beyond the statue of Paul Revere stands the historic church, its tower rebuilt after having been destroyed by Hurricane Carol in 1954. Funds for the restoration were raised by school children all over the United States.

"By the rude bridge that arched the flood,
Their flag to April's breeze unfurled,
Here once the embattled farmers stood
And fired the shot heard round the world.'

The "rude bridge" across the Concord River, made famous in Ralph Waldo Emerson's lines, has been accurately rebuilt in recent years.

Legions of visitors cross the bridge to see the Minuteman statue, first important work of Daniel Chester French, the New England sculptor whose greatest work is the statue of Abraham Lincoln in Washington. The Minuteman is familiar to everyone who recalls its use as a symbol during World War II.

"The hills were reared, the valleys scooped in vain,
If Learning's altars vanish from the plain."

WILLIAM ELLERY CHANNING

As a symbol for
LEARNING IN NEW ENGLAND we have selected the Bullet Hill School in Southbury, Connecticut, built in 1778 or before, and considered one of the oldest New England schools in continuous use.

The one-room rural schoolhouse still flourishes in the New England hills. This nostalgic example is in Gassetts, Vermont.

Some of the free academies that were founded and maintained by New England towns in the 18th and 19th centuries are still in operation. A fine example is the North Yarmouth Academy *(opposite)*, founded in 1810 in North Yarmouth, Maine. Its pedimented brick buildings are vine-grown, crested with delicate white towers.

This small red schoolhouse set in a grove of pines is said to be the one attended by Mary Sawyer, who was the heroine of the classic verse, "Mary Had A Little Lamb." Built in 1798, the school was being used as a garage when Henry Ford purchased it in 1927 and moved it to a site near the Wayside Inn at South Sudbury, Massachusetts.

92

Phillips Exeter Academy was opened in Exeter, New Hampshire, in 1783, its benefactor being John Phillips. A graduate of Harvard at sixteen, he tried teaching and then commerce, at which he succeeded handsomely. He also sponsored an academy in Andover with his brother, and there has always been a strenuous rivalry between the two schools. Above is a view of the Academy Building, central unit of a large campus.

Phillips Andover Academy for boys in Andover, Massachusetts *(opposite)*, is the oldest incorporated school in America, being established in 1778 by Samuel Phillips. Among the Academy's hundred or more buildings are two designed by the great Boston architect, Charles Bulfinch. One of them, built in 1818, is named Bulfinch Hall in his honor.

Lenox Academy occupies a graceful old building in the Berkshire resort town of Lenox, Massachusetts. Its Palladian window and wide pedimented doorway are quite sensitive in design. The celebrated Tanglewood Music Festival is held nearby.

St. Paul's School, built over a hundred years ago on a beautiful site outside of Concord, New Hampshire, is one of America's most exclusive preparatory schools. Most of its buildings are Georgian Colonial in style, but the brick Gothic chapel is reminiscent of rural England.

The architecture of an ancient, sagging Cotswold community is simulated in Avon Old Farms School, at Avon, Connecticut (*opposite*). After World War II it served for a time as a hospital for blinded war veterans.

Perhaps the most exclusive of all New England schools is Groton, established in 1884 on a 90-acre farm by the Reverend Endicott Peabody, in Groton, Massachusetts. His ambition was to form "an Episcopal School where the Headmaster, as in England, was also the pastor." Franklin D. Roosevelt was a distinguished alumnus of the school.

96

A fine Gothic tower looms over St. George's School near Newport, Rhode Island. Founded in 1896 by the Reverend John Diman, its tree-shaded campus affords a superb view of the shore and Rhode Island Sound. The Chapel, dedicated in 1928, is one of the finest examples of English Gothic design in the country.

Kent School is beautifully situated on the banks of the Housatonic River at Kent, Connecticut. It is an Episcopal school, founded by the much esteemed Father Sill in 1906. Kent is famous for its crews, which have come back victorious from the Henley Regatta in England on many occasions.

Oldest and greatest of American universities, Harvard was established in Cambridge, Massachusetts, in 1636 when the General Court agreed to give 400 pounds to a school or college. At that time John Harvard, a young minister from Charlestown, died, bequeathing his library and one-half of his estate (in all about 1700 pounds) to the proposed college. It was decreed that the new college should bear John Harvard's name. The Court also changed the name of the town, naming it after the old university city of Cambridge, England.

Foremost among the country's technological colleges, the Massachusetts Institute of Technology recently celebrated its first century. Founded in Boston in 1861, it moved across the Charles River to Cambridge in 1916.

Spring date at Yale. Towering over the old campus in New Haven, Connecticut, is the Harkness Tower *(opposite),* superb example of collegiate Gothic designed by James Gamble Rogers and completed in 1921.

Brown University, seventh oldest in the country, was founded in 1764 in Warren, Rhode Island, and was originally named Rhode Island College. It was moved to Providence in 1770 when the "College Edifice," now known as University Hall, was built. During the Revolution classes were suspended, and this fine brick building was used as a barracks by French and American troops. In 1804 the University was renamed in recognition of an endowment from Nicholas Brown.

Facing the college green in Hanover, New Hampshire *(opposite)*, are three sunlit buildings that are dear to all Dartmouth men—Wentworth, Dartmouth, and Bissell halls. The central building is a fireproof replica of the original Dartmouth Hall, built in 1791 and destroyed by fire in 1904.

Trinity College in Hartford, Connecticut, was incorporated in 1823 as Washington College, adopting its present name in 1845. Its beautiful Gothic chapel, built in 1932, is very English in feeling, and has an outdoor pulpit.

103

Williams College *(upper left)* was founded by the will of Colonel Ephriam Williams, who was killed in the French and Indian War. It was chartered many years later as Williams College, and it has always remained small and exclusive. Here is Griffin Hall, a fine Federal building, named for the third president of the college. The chapel tower is in the foreground.

Another small college for men, Amherst *(upper right)* has the great advantage of being within courting distance of Smith College. Between two rather severe dormitories is a time-honored landmark, Johnson Chapel, with a fine Doric portico and white clock tower. Calvin Coolidge was one of Amherst's distinguished sons.

Smith College, in Northampton, Massachusetts, is architecturally a bit distraught, but it does have some handsome dormitory quadrangles. In 1875 Sophia Smith, a resident of Hatfield, established this college for "the intelligent gentlewoman." Beginning with fourteen students at that time, it has grown to be one of the largest and most respected colleges in the country.

Radcliffe College in Cambridge, Massachusetts, was organized in 1879, and is affiliated with Harvard. This is the Radcliffe Yard.

Good collegiate Gothic flourishes at Mt. Holyoke College for Women, founded in 1837 at North Hadley, Massachusetts.

Connecticut College for Women occupies a spacious campus at New London, Connecticut. This is the Harkness Chapel.

Wellesley College in Wellesley, Massachusetts, founded in 1871, once favored the Gothic tradition, but its newer buildings are handsomely modern.

Colby College, occupying a hillside campus on the outskirts of Waterville, Maine, is distinguished by formal Georgian buildings of contemporary design. The original college dates from the early 19th century when a school of theology was founded in Waterville by the Reverend Jeremiah Chaplin with seven students. Named in honor of an early benefactor, it has been coeducational since 1871.

Bowdoin College in Brunswick, Maine, was named in honor of the wealthy James Bowdoin, Governor of Massachusetts, whose son responded to the honor by contributing generously to the college. Classes began in this three-story brick building called Massachusetts Hall in 1802. The president's office is now here, located in what was once the college kitchen. Exclusively a men's institution, Bowdoin has always been a center for intellectual and literary celebrities. Some of the famous men connected with it are Nathaniel Hawthorne; Henry Wadsworth Longfellow; Rear Admiral Robert E. Perry; Franklin Pierce, 14th President of the United States; and Donald B. MacMillan, Arctic explorer.

One of the newer women's colleges, Bennington *(upper left)* occupies a beautiful hillside site above the town of Bennington, Vermont. It was opened in 1932 and has gained remarkable prestige in its short existence, particularly in the field of the arts. This is the central college hall.

The coeducational University of Vermont at Burlington *(upper right)* was united with the State Agricultural College in 1865. At the right is the Billings Library, built in 1885, and considered to be one of the masterpieces of H. H. Richardson. In the background is the campanile of the Ira Allen Chapel with four clock faces and a powerful electric beacon.

Chartered in Middlebury, Vermont, in 1800, Middlebury College is a marble-built college for men and women with an especially fine reputation for its English and foreign language summer schools. Topped by a graceful white tower, the Old Chapel, built in 1836, now functions as the Administration building. In the foreground is the first college dormitory, Starr Hall, built in 1861.

Schools of a different kind are these. Above is the School of Philosophy, a small wooden Gothic building that served for almost a decade as Bronson Alcott's summer school of Philosophy in Concord, Massachusetts. Located on a slope above Orchard House, the Alcott home, this school was the main preoccupation of father Alcott while his wife and daughters worked bravely to balance the family budget. Louisa May Alcott's very successful books solved the problem.

The first law school in America was founded in this small building in Litchfield, Connecticut, by Tapping Reeve, in 1784. Reeve's wife was the sister of Aaron Burr, who became one of the first law students. The list of graduates from this small law school is impressive. It contains six cabinet members, two vice-presidents, twenty-eight United States senators, and 101 other members of Congress, not to mention ten governors and three justices of the Supreme Court.

EARLY INNS AND TAVERNS still adorn the New England roadside, particularly on Cape Cod. Old Yarmouth Inn has presumably been greeting travelers in Yarmouthport, Massachusetts, since 1696.

The Buckman Tavern (1690), facing the Battle Green in Lexington, Massachusetts, was the scene of great excitement on the morning of April 19, 1775. Minutemen gathered around the great fireplace in the taproom to await word of the British advance, and Paul Revere saw them arrive from a tavern window. Two wounded British soldiers received first aid here; one died, and was buried in the old cemetery. The first village store and post office were located here.

The Old Hayden Tavern (1766) in the maritime village of Essex, Connecticut *(opposite),* was originally owned by Uriah Hayden, a leading shipbuilder and merchant of his time. The building now serves as a club.

The famous taproom and bar of the Buckman Tavern have been preserved just as they appeared on the first day of the Revolution.

110

Longfellow's Wayside Inn at South Sudbury, Massachusetts, has recently been rebuilt after a serious fire in the winter of 1955. Built in 1686 by Samuel Howe, a most gifted landlord, the old inn catered to the needs of stagecoach passengers for centuries. Five generations by the name of Howe served as hosts. Henry Ford Sr. first purchased and restored the Wayside Inn in 1923. This is the way it looks at present, with a group of antique automobiles occupying the driveway for the day.

The Samuel Hartwell House in Lincoln, Massachusetts, now known as the Hartwell Farm, is one of the surviving houses that lay along Battle Road between Lexington and Concord. Red-coated Grenadiers marched past on the morning of April 19, 1775, and returned in disarray the same night. In recent years the Hartwell Farm has been converted into a charming rural restaurant.

Most NEW ENGLAND MILLS are inclined to be austere. Not so this wooden mill on the Blackstone River in Pawtucket, Rhode Island, built by the first successful makers of cotton thread in America. It was Samuel Slater, a young Englishman, who brought the secret of spinning to Pawtucket. This mill is named for him and still contains some of the original machinery he designed.

At a dam on the Squannacook River in Townsend Harbor, Massachusetts, is Spaulding's Grist Mill, built about 1840. Its ancient wooden and wrought-iron machinery is still in fine condition.

On the grounds of Longfellow's Wayside Inn *(opposite)* a stone grist mill has been built on 18th-century lines. It is powered by an overshot water wheel. Unbleached flour and cereal are ground between old circular burr stones and sold to interested visitors.

The Wight Grist Mill has a 20-foot undershot water wheel that is turned by water flowing under the road. This mill was moved from Hebron, Connecticut, to form a part of Old Sturbridge Village. A conversational miller is on hand to explain the intricacies of his profession.

The first ironworks in America was founded in 1641 by John Winthrop Jr., who sailed from England with a group of skilled iron workers and installed a forge in Saugus, Massachusetts. The town then bore the appropriate name of Hammersmith. The Saugus Ironworks has been carefully reconstructed in recent years, and visitors may now see how primitive blast furnaces and water wheels functioned. The first fire engine in America supposedly came from this plant.

*"Cut down trees in the forest
And build me a wooden house."*

RALPH WALDO EMERSON

The pictorial essay on
OLD NEW ENGLAND HOUSES begins with
the Short House (1733) in Old Newbury, Massachusetts.

The Fairbanks House in Dedham, Massachusetts, is believed by many to be the oldest frame structure now standing in the country. It was built in 1636 with oak timbers brought from England. Since Jonathan Fayerbanke occupied the house with his wife and six children, only one family, the Fairbanks, has lived in it. In 325 years it has never been deeded or mortgaged.

The Parson Capen House in Topsfield, Massachusetts *(opposite)*, is one of the most flawless examples of the English manor house in this country. It is thought to have been built by craftsmen freshly arrived from England. It has a pilastered brick chimney, leaded windows, and wooden pendants under its wide overhang, all Elizabethan features. It was built by the Reverend Joseph Capen in 1683 as a gift to his bride.

The Old Ironworks House in Saugus is another striking example of a gabled Elizabethan manor house. It was built about 1643 by Thomas Dexter, one of the owners of the neighboring ironworks. According to tradition, the first designs for the Pine Tree and Oak Tree shillings were made in this house. The building was restored in recent years by Wallace Nutting. Now furnished with 17th-century pieces, it forms a part of the museum group known as the Saugus Ironworks.

Built about 1660 in Farmington, Connecticut, the Samuel Whitman House is a most unusual "saltbox" with a massive stone chimney and wide framed overhang. The overhang had value in England, as it offered some protection from the rain, but it served poorly in the rugged New England weather, and was soon abandoned.

The McIntire Garrison House (opposite), built between 1640 and 1645, stands in open country near York, Maine. Its overhang, which extends on all four sides, permitted beleaguered settlers to pour hot pitch and grease upon Indian attackers.

This vine-grown gambrel-roofed cottage in Plymouth, Massachusetts, is the historic Harlow House, built in 1677 with timbers taken from the old Pilgrim fort on Burial Hill.

The oldest stone house in New England was built in 1639 in Guilford, Connecticut, by the Reverend Henry Whitfield, founder of the town. Burned out in the 19th century, the old house has been restored to its early state in recent years, and is now open to the public.

The Amasa Gray House *(opposite)* is one of New England's most picturesque structures, built on the highway outside of Little Compton, Rhode Island. An early "block house," it was built by early settlers, William and Sarah Dye, in 1684. Several wings have since been added.

The Atwood House, oldest in Chatham, Massachusetts, was built in 1752 by Joseph Atwood, "a navigator of unfrequented parts." Not a typical Cape Cod cottage, it has a gambrel roof, which allows for a roomier second story.

The gambrel-roofed cottage is a device that permits a great deal of room in what appears to be a limited space. This fine one in Old Lyme, Connecticut, believed to date from 1726, is a very pure unsymmetrical example. Old Lyme is a sleepy, elm-shaded town, steeped in the seafaring tradition. One can easily imagine a sea captain returning to this cottage after a long voyage.

The old pitch-roofed cottage begins to appear long before one reaches Cape Cod. This inviting example, whose dormers may be a little larger than usual, is found in Hingham, Massachusetts.

Orford, New Hampshire, is a superb New England village with a string of noble 18th-century houses set well back from the road. One of them was designed by Charles Bulfinch, and the others follow his example, including this little hip-roofed house. Washington Irving wrote this of Orford: "In all my travels in this country and Europe I have never seen any village more beautiful than this."

Rebecca Nurse, an innocent and courageous woman, was taken from this house and hanged as a witch in 1692 during the Salem witchcraft delusion. The house was built in Danvers, Massachusetts, by her husband, Francis Nurse. The favored chair of the martyred woman, mother of nine, is on exhibition here. Nearby is her grave and a monument with an inscription composed by John Greenleaf Whittier.

125

"Forty Acres," the Porter-Phelps-Huntington House, was built in 1752 on the banks of the Connecticut River, near Hadley, Massachusetts. This serene Colonial mansion, now open to the public, has been in the Huntington family for ten generations, and has remained untouched for more than a century and a half.

The Frary House in Old Deerfield, Massachusetts *(opposite),* is the sole survivor of the tragic fire and massacre that swept over this village in 1704. Built in the 1680's by Samson Frary (who was murdered in the massacre), it became an inn during the 18th century and a favorite meeting place of the local Whigs. Benedict Arnold came here in May 1775 in a colonel's uniform to buy beef for the army then forming. The house is now handsomely furnished and open to the public.

This view of a typical New England farmhouse in Carlisle, Massachusetts, is framed by a stone wall and a burst of golden autumn foliage.

An old saltbox house in Essex County, Massachusetts, is set in the trappings of a New England winter. It glows with warmth and comfort and good cheer despite the cold weather.

The "Wedding Cake House" *(opposite)* in Kennebunk, Maine, is a reminder of the scroll-saw era. A simple two-story brick house has been transformed by grotesque Gothic gingerbread, to effect an architectural valentine.

Putnam Cottage, built in Greenwich, Connecticut, in 1731, is maintained as a museum by the D.A.R. It still retains its rounded-end shingles. Tradition has it that General Israel Putnam escaped from this house, originally known as Knapp's Tavern, when the Redcoats approached it in 1779. He jumped astride his horse and vanished safely over a rocky precipice.

The residence of the president of Williams College, in Williamstown, Massachusetts, is a handsomely designed Federal house with a formal classic façade. The central motif consists of a Palladian window above an Ionic columned doorway. This is flanked by tall pilasters and surmounted by a roof railing decorated with urns.

Rising along Nantucket's cobble-stoned Main Street are three identical Georgian mansions known locally as "West Brick," "Middle Brick," and "East Brick." They were built in the late 1830's by Joseph Starbuck for his three sons, George, Matthew, and William, and they still stand in prim, well-groomed serenity.

The Adams Mansion in Quincy, Massachusetts, was the home of both Presidents John Adams and John Quincy Adams. Built in 1731 by Major John Vassall, it is a large sprawling building with a lovely garden. John Adams purchased it in 1787, and here he entertained Lafayette in 1824. It is now the Adams Family Memorial, and open to the public.

The home of Colonel Jeremiah Lee of Washington's Army, this impressive mansion is one of the country's finest. Built in the old town of Marblehead, Massachusetts, in 1768, it is said to have cost its prosperous owner ten thousand pre-Revolutionary pounds. Its central stair hall is magnificently wide. Two fine sets of paper hangings were made especially for it in England.

On a hilltop overlooking the town of Thomaston, Maine, is the replica of "Montpelier," the original home of Major General Henry Knox. The celebrated soldier, who died as the result of swallowing a chicken bone, lived for many years in Thomaston. The house contains his furniture and personal effects.

132

The John Paul Jones House in Portsmouth, New Hampshire, is a gambrel-roofed dwelling built in 1758 by Captain Gregory Purcell. When the captain died in 1776, leaving a widow and seven children, she kept this as a rooming house. Among her lodgers was John Paul Jones who was in Portsmouth to supervise the building of the *Ranger,* and later the *America.* The house has been restored by the local historical society.

The Maria Mitchell House is a typical unsymmetrical Nantucket dwelling, built in 1790. Here the first woman astronomer was born in 1818, and here she carried out her experiments with the heavens. She became a teacher of astronomy at Vassar and received many honors, discovered several comets, and was given a gold medal by the King of Denmark. Her observatory and stark little house are now visited by thousands of "off-islanders."

133

The Nichols-Lee House, one of the seven famous mansions of "Tory Row" in Cambridge, dates from 1660. During the Revolution it was occupied by Joseph Lee, a much respected judge.

The elegant façade of the John Brown House *(opposite)*, built in 1786 in Providence, Rhode Island, gives a hint of the architectural richness to be found within. It was built in the Federal style for John Brown, merchant prince, and designed by his architect brother, Joseph Brown. George Washington visited the house in 1790 and drank a glass of punch with his host.

The Governor Langdon House, built in 1784 in Portsmouth, New Hampshire, was the home of the town's most distinguished patriot, John Langdon. He became in turn a delegate to the Continental Congress, signer of the Constitution, and President of the United States Senate.

The Royall House in Medford, Massachusetts, is built around an original farmhouse said to have been built by Governor Winthrop in the 1630's. The present "nobleman's house" dates from 1732, and was used as headquarters for Stark's division during the Revolution. Here General Washington met with his generals to plan the siege of Boston.

The Black House in Ellsworth, Maine, is a charming brick country residence built with two wings in the early 1800's. Colonel John Black, its builder, was a land agent who lavished a fortune on it. Surrounded by beautiful grounds, it is a museum house, open to the public.

The Elisha Payne House (1815) in the little town of Canterbury, Connecticut, is a smiling, pedimented building with a fine Palladian window. It was run as a "select" school by Prudence Crandall, a Quaker, who precipitated a national controversy by admitting a small colored girl. The school teacher finally gave up and fled when irate citizens stoned her house.

The Pierce-Nichols House is one of the earliest and best examples of the genius of the great carver-architect, Samuel McIntire. It was built in Salem, Massachusetts, in 1782 by Jerathmiel Pierce, wealthy East India merchant, whose ships were loaded on a dock at the rear of this mansion.

Gore Place in Waltham, Massachusetts, is one of America's truly great houses. It was built in 1802–4 by Christopher Gore, patriot, lawyer, Chargé d'Affaires in London, and Governor of the Commonwealth. This brick mansion with a bow front and wide-stretched wings looked out on broad and peaceful acres, now somewhat diminished in size. In recent years the mansion has been rescued from its role of country club and it is now preserved for posterity.

The spacious Blaine Mansion in Augusta, Maine, was built about 1830 in the Classical Revival tradition. James G. Blaine, "the plumed knight of politics," purchased the house in 1862, and here he learned of his nomination for the Presidency in 1876. The house now serves as the Executive Mansion for the Governor.

Linden Place, better known as the Colt Mansion, was built in Bristol, Rhode Island, in 1810 by George De Wolfe. With a massive Corinthian portico, it is one of the most ambitious of post-Colonial houses in New England.

140

BUILT BY
ENEZER GRANT
1757

There is infinite variety in
NEW ENGLAND DOORWAYS. Here, for example, is the pure Connecticut Valley type
embellishing the façade of the Ebenezer Grant House in East Windsor, Connecticut. Its broken
pediment is strongly Jacobean in feeling, and the door itself is elaborately paneled.

A perfect Georgian doorway with a fifteen-paneled door graces the Wentworth-Gardiner House (1760) in Portsmouth, New Hampshire.

A sophisticated semi-elliptical Corinthian portico appears on the Pingree House (1810) in Salem.

This fine double-pilastered portico is the entrance to a house in Salem designed by Samuel McIntire.

The unusual cornice detail of this doorway in Duxbury, Massachusetts, is in the best Cape Cod tradition.

Great delicacy is evident in the iron railing, fanlight, and columns of this doorway on Beacon Street, Boston.

The unpainted doorway of the John Williams House (1707) in Old Deerfield, Massachusetts, is in the Connecticut Valley tradition.

A series of arches supported by slender Corinthian columns marks this graceful Federal doorway in Castleton, Vermont.

An elliptical fanlight and sidelights brighten this doorway on a hillside mansion in Providence, Rhode Island

The welcoming approach to the Nickels-Sortwell House in Wiscasset, Maine, is one of the most beautiful of all New England doorways. The broken portico, slightly bowed and supported by slender Corinthian columns, is unmatched. The terrace railing lends a final touch of distinction. Built in 1807–12 by Captain William Nickels, this house later became a tavern, but is now restored to its original beauty.

This abbreviated portfolio of
NEW ENGLAND INTERIORS begins at Timestone Farm, a remarkably unchanged
17th-century house in Marlboro, Massachusetts. In the corner of the dining room is a four-
post bed, quite the customary place for overnight guests or family in those days. The center
table, an early dropleaf duckfoot type, is supplied with bread, cheese, and wine.

The Pembroke room at Beauport, the remarkable house of many periods at Gloucester, Massachusetts, is filled with early pine pieces. A massive wooden lintel spans the fireplace.

A finely paneled corner cupboard *(opposite)* appears in an old house in Darien, Connecticut. A Queen Anne chair and candlestand complete the group.

The kitchen of the John Ward House (1684) in Salem, Massachusetts, recreates the atmosphere of the 17th century down to the smallest detail. Pewter and wooden plates rest on the table and pine dresser.

The Richard Derby House, built at the head of famous Derby Wharf in Salem in 1762, is a fine example of a brick Colonial house. The paneled interiors are painted in rich, muted colors. This house is now part of a museum group administered by the Department of the Interior.

This handsomely paneled room *(opposite above)* is in the Mission House in Stockbridge, Massachusetts. It was built in 1739 for John Sergeant, the young Yale tutor who became the first missionary to the Housatonic Indians.

The Hogarth Room *(opposite below)* in the Allen House in Deerfield, Massachusetts, is adorned with many Hogarth prints and two portraits by John Singleton Copley. Both the gateleg table and armchair have Spanish feet.

The ballroom in the Hall Tavern in Old Deerfield *(right)* was heated by a single fireplace, decorated with stencilling by an anonymous but very whimsical artist. One fireplace in a ballroom seems hardly enough on a winter night, but then square dancers furnish their own warmth.

149

The east bedroom of the Pierce-Nichols House in Salem is dominated by a four-post bed that belonged to the Nichols family. Their leather-covered camphor wood chest sits at the foot of the bed.

One of the most luxurious of Colonial mansions *(opposite above)* was built in 1768 by Colonel Jeremiah Lee in Marblehead, Massachusetts. The state chamber still retains the original landscape paper that was painted for it in England.

The Moffat-Ladd House *(opposite below),* built in Portsmouth, New Hampshire, in 1763, is embellished with a remarkable stair hall. The stairway has a richly ornamented soffit, and on the wall is a fine example of the "Bay of Naples" paper, originally printed in Paris.

The wheat sheaf *(left)* was the most individual and personal of all of Samuel McIntire's carved devices. His superb ability as a woodcarver can be observed in this mantel detail in the Pingree House, built in Salem, Massachusetts, in 1804.

150

The State Dining Room at Gore Place in Waltham, Massachusetts, is imposing in its scale and simplicity, a handsome example of the Federal period. The great men of Governor Gore's day were entertained here, among them Lafayette, Talleyrand, Adams, Monroe, and Daniel Webster. The architect is unknown, but many critics think it was Charles Bulfinch.

In the central hallway of the Peirce Mansion (1799) in Portsmouth, New Hampshire (*opposite*), is an elliptical staircase climbing up two flights in a graceful spiral. The mahogany Hepplewhite settle fits so perfectly that it must have been built expressly for this place. The crossed duelling swords of a distant ancestor hang on the wall.

Four Hepplewhite chairs surround a card table in the front parlor of the Pingree House in Salem, McIntire's triumph in his later years. This superb three-story mansion expresses the restrained opulence that marked the homes of wealthy merchants and ship owners in Salem's great days.

The West Parlor of the Vassall-Craigie-Longfellow House in Cambridge is furnished with Victorian pieces of Longfellow's day. He occupied the house for forty-five years, up to his death in 1882.

The central hallway of the Sarah Orne Jewett House (1774) in South Berwick, Maine, reveals fine wood carving and a graceful stairway. The noted authoress of *The Country of the Pointed Firs* was born and died in this house.

154

This pictorial essay closes with a journey up the
NEW ENGLAND COAST from Connecticut to the far coastal corner of Maine. The most
famous vessel along the Connecticut shore is the *Charles W. Morgan,* the last of the whalers, which was towed to a final mooring at Mystic Seaport, Connecticut, in 1941. A veteran
of thirty-seven long whaling expeditions across the seven seas, she is but one of the attractions
of this revived seaport community.

The Connecticut shore is marked by many picturesque waterside towns such as Niantic, shown in this picture. The trappings are almost always the same—a pole wharf, marine railway, and a scattering of lobster pots, fishing boats, and pleasure craft. The town fishermen in Niantic have been bringing in scallops since the 17th century.

A drama of sea and sky surrounds the Saybrook Lighthouse, built in 1866 at the mouth of the Connecticut River. Offshore waters provide fine snapper bluefishing in August and September.

Stonington, Connecticut, first settled in 1649, has been for centuries a successful fishing port extending into Block Island Sound. Bluefish, swordfish, and haddock are brought in by swarthy mariners, many of them of Portuguese ancestry. Fishing gear and lobster traps clutter the docks, and seagulls lend noise and color.

The old lighthouse at the end of Stonington's peninsula is a squat granite building whose white paint has almost washed away. It now serves as a museum for Stonington's many summer visitors.

The rocky perimeter of New-port, Rhode Island, offers the intrepid fisherman many opportunities for surf casting.

Wickford, Rhode Island *(opposite)*, is not only a village of great architectural charm but also a miniature seaport in great favor with yachtsmen and professional fishermen. This square-rigged sailing vessel lends particular charm to Wickford's docks.

Sakonnet, a fishing hamlet at the far lower extremity of Rhode Island, has suffered cruelly from two hurricanes, but has always rebuilt valiantly.

Menemsha is a remote fishing village on the western extremity of the island of Martha's Vineyard. It is populated almost entirely by amphibious fishermen-farmers. Its miniature fishing port is enclosed by a spit populated with functional wooden houses that are replaced after each hurricane.

Gay Head *(opposite)*, the westernmost extremity of Martha's Vineyard, is the most colorful and dramatic part of the island. Here reflected in the wet sands, the multicolored promontory becomes a symphony of rich tone, particularly in the late afternoon. Native Indians have always made up the greater part of the population of this seaside hamlet.

Vineyard Haven, the town with the largest year-round population on Martha's Vineyard, has a protected harbor that has for centuries been a refuge for sailing craft in threatening weather. This peaceful view shows the ferryboat that connects the island with Cape Cod. The island was named by Bartholomew Gosnold, the explorer, in 1602. Just who Martha was, nobody seems to know.

The immensity of the nearby Atlantic is sensed in the flat reaches of Madaket, at the western end of Nantucket Island.

Nantucket, a romantic outpost on the Atlantic, was at one time the world's greatest whaling port. It was settled by the white man in the middle of the 17th century, when the island was populated by several hundred Indians who gained a livelihood by fishing and farming. Sheep raising was a principal industry until the 18th century, when whaling came into its own. Nantucket's sperm candles were shipped all over the world, and its sailors traveled just as far. Today the island is the haven of the summer visitor and the fortunate retired businessman who lives here the year around. The neat little shingled buildings on the Nantucket docks include the exclusive Wharf Rats Club *(opposite)*, with the likeness of a whale for its weathervane.

Several windmills once stood on a gentle dune south of the town of Nantucket, but only this one, "East Mill," remains. It was built in 1746, partly with timbers from wrecked vessels. Nathan Wilbur, its builder, also designed the machinery which is still in fine running order.

163

Cape Cod has no greater splendor than this—the matchless expanse of sandy shore that runs in a bold fifty-mile crescent to the tip of Provincetown. Bathers are particularly happy at Nauset Beach, near Orleans.

The great open feeling of Cape Cod is evident in this view of the wind-swept dunes at Eastham *(opposite above)*, an area that only recently has been declared a national seashore. This region was explored in 1606 by Samuel de Champlain, and settled in 1644.

On the exposed outer shores of Provincetown *(opposite below)* many wrecks have been cast up in recent generations. Their life on the sands is a short one, for they all seem to vanish in a few brief years.

The essence of Cape Cod is summed up in this view just north of the town of Chatham *(right)*—a fisherman's dock built up with neat shingled buildings trimmed in white, lobster pots galore, and a distant sand spit.

165

In 1620 the *Mayflower*, bound for Virginia, was blown off her course and finally landed in the dangerous shoals of Cape Cod. She anchored first at what is now Provincetown, but after a month the Pilgrims landed in Plymouth Harbor, shown here. Tied up in the same harbor is the replica of the original *Mayflower*, recently built in England and sailed to America. After attracting visitors in many maritime cities, the colorful sailing vessel is now a permanent part of Plimouth Plantation, a praiseworthy museum project.

The U.S. Frigate *Constitution (opposite)*, better known as "Old Ironsides," is moored in the United States Navy Yard in Charlestown, Massachusetts. This view shows her bowsprit, with the former training ship *Nantucket* drying her sails in the distance.

The imposing Doric monument that shelters Plymouth Rock dwarfs the rock itself, two-thirds of which is under the sand. Popular sentiment holds to the tradition that the first group of Pilgrims landed on this rock, regardless of the arched eyebrows of many historians.

The famous T-Wharf in Boston *(opposite)* is usually a clutter of gaudily painted fishing vessels, often with Italian or Portuguese crews. The Boston Custom House stands impassively above this animated scene.

This is a pure case of photographer's luck. One of the last of the old three-masted coastal schooners was caught drying her sails while her crew unloaded lumber in Lynn, Massachusetts.

"The Yachting Capital of the Eastern Seaboard" is the title that Marblehead, Massachusetts, carries gracefully on its shoulders. During Race Week *(above)* its white sails can be counted in the hundreds.

Rockport, Massachusetts, is the most conspicuous haven of the summer artist along this coast, and this is his favorite subject—an old red fish house referred to as "Motif Number One."

The craft of the old shipwrights who shaped these wooden ribs and keel is fast disappearing along this coast. This pleasant scene occurred in Essex, Massachusetts, setting of the old Storey shipyards, founded in 1668. Their ways were once crowded with "Chebacco boats" of the old Cape Ann fishermen, together with trawlers, schooners, and yachts.

The broad Atlantic is here, breaking peacefully on Bass Rocks in Massachusetts on a clear summer afternoon. The scene is far more ominous during a winter storm.

171

Gloucester, Massachusetts, the pioneer fishing town of America three hundred years ago, is still one of the most active fishing ports in the country, and one of the most paintable. There is boundless animation at the water's edge, accompanied by the chatter of many tongues. On a misty April morning there is a certain mystery, too.

Portrait of a lighthouse (*opposite*). Annisquam, Massachusetts.

A study of Gloucester's drying nets. Barely visible on the horizon is the spire of the first Universalist Church in America.

Lanesville, Massachusetts, on the northern tip of Cape Ann, is a miniature fishing port protected by sturdy walls of granite blocks, and still used by a small, hard-bitten group of fishermen.

New Hampshire's "brief but distinguished shoreline" *(opposite)* is bordered with miles of sandy beaches and a succession of summer settlements. The vapor trails in the sky indicate that an Air Force base is situated nearby.

The silhouette of Newburyport, Massachusetts, has changed but little in the past century. The old brick warehouses and stone docks on the banks of the Merrimac River and the graceful church spires appear totally unchanged. But Newburyport's day as a great port has faded.

A misty morning near the mouth of the Piscataqua River at Portsmouth, New Hampshire. Explorers were in this area at the dawn of the 17th century. In 1603 Martin Pring and his crew sailed two ships up the river in search of—sassafras.

One of the miniature harbors along the New Hampshire shore is at Rye North Beach, whose unpretentious Yacht Club is marked by a shingled second-story lookout.

176

Everything in this picture of Kittery Harbor bespeaks the coast of Maine—offshore islands, a clipper-bowed schooner with her dark sails up to dry, fishing boats and dories at the float, and the brilliant light so typical of this coast.

Nubble Light, at York, Maine, is different from most lighthouses. It is on an offshore island, and the peaceful Coast Guard lads who take care of it are undisturbed by tourists.

Things have changed in Boothbay Harbor, Maine, since this picture was taken a quarter of a century ago. Several idle coastal schooners were moored in its harbor at that time, but now all of them have vanished to an uncertain fate.

A secluded inlet at Thomaston, Maine *(opposite)*, once played host to the *Reine Marie Stuart,* a famous square-rigged schooner. She has also disappeared, as have the little wooden shacks in the foreground which were used for smoking alewives.

Some Maine lobstermen are very conscious of the photogenic qualities of their waterside abodes. One obliging resident of Cape Porpoise, Maine, keeps his house bedecked with colorful markers that invariably attract the passing photographer. Lobster pots dominate the foreground.

Portland Head Light is the oldest lighthouse on the Maine coast, built in 1791. Rising over a hundred feet above the water, it casts its warning light far out to sea.

Even the camera can paint a picture when the subject is as beguiling as this view of Kittery Point, Maine *(opposite)*. Local lobstermen still use this tiny port the year around.

The Crescent, Prout's Neck, Maine. This fashionable summer settlement near Scarboro enjoys a wide sandy beach of great appeal.

From the hillside at Sullivan, Maine, the passing traveler has a superb view across Frenchman Bay to Mount Desert, dominated by the conical silhouette of Cadillac Mountain.

Camden is one of Maine's most beautiful towns, lying at the base of the Camden Hills, and enclosing a deep harbor which is given over to private yachts and fishing schooners that have been converted into summer cruise boats. These "dude ships" are most popular with big city visitors.

For decades Wiscasset's harbor has sheltered two sagging derelicts whose condition has grown progressively more forlorn as the years go by. This detailed view shows the prow of the *Luther Little* at the beginning of her decline.

The easternmost point in the United States is called, perversely enough, West Quoddy Head. Here a Coast Guard station and a red-and-white-striped lighthouse look out on the Grand Manan Channel. In the distance is a first glimpse of Canada—Campobello Island, where Franklin D. Roosevelt maintained his summer home.

(Overleaf) Port Clyde, Maine.

INDEX